George B. Taylor

Man's best friend, the dog;

A treatise upon the dog

.

George B. Taylor

Man's best friend, the dog;
A treatise upon the dog

ISBN/EAN: 9783337814915

Printed in Europe, USA, Canada, Australia, Japan

Cover: Foto ©ninafisch / pixelio.de

More available books at **www.hansebooks.com**

MAN'S FRIEND, THE DOG

A TREATISE UPON THE DOG, WITH INFORMATION AS TO
THE VALUE OF THE DIFFERENT BREEDS, AND
THE BEST WAY TO CARE FOR THEM

BY

GEORGE B. TAYLOR

NEW YORK
FREDERICK A. STOKES COMPANY
MDCCCXCI

CONTENTS.

DEDICATION.

To the Westminster Kennel Club of 1877, the women who were exhibitors at its first Bench Show, Charles Lincoln, the Rev. J. Cumming Macdona, William Lort, Esq., F. R. G. S., and to all whose efforts to improve and elevate the dog have been crowned with such eminent success, this unconventional treatise is dedicated.

INTRODUCTION.

"Between two dogs * * * * * *
Good faith I am no more than a daw."

Henry VI.

THIS little work will not treat of the dog, man's dumb friend, as a sporting or a fighting animal, but will discuss it as a companion of the human race and a guardian and ornament of the home. Those who delight in the pugnacity of certain breeds and the cultivators of "freak" dogs are not friends of the noble animal and have no place here.

The author is mindful of Shakespeare's caption, but if you possess a dog, gentle reader, you may in these chapters discover how the better to care for it. If you contemplate owning one, remember "Mr. Punch's" "advice to young persons about to marry, 'Don't'!"

Do not own a dog—unless you are prepared to treat it, in a certain sense, as one of the family, to give it "All the comforts of home" and, in more ways than one, be its patient, faithful servant. Be also prepared to submit to not a little inconvenience in shaping out its daily life in order that, instead of a nuisance, it may become a healthy, joyous creature that will have a lasting hold on your affections.

MAN'S FRIEND, THE DOG.

THE IMPROVED TASTE IN DOGS.

AMERICA is becoming nice in matters canine; she has got beyond the "Peter Bell," the "yellow primrose" period of fifteen years ago. There was a time, and not so very long since, that newspaper wits—Heaven save the mark!—made the columns of the press less dreary with stories in which the stock *dramatis-personae* were invariably a kicking mule, a fool, a "gal," an old sinner and—"a yaller purp." Bench shows have done much to give old and young object lessons in respect for the once despised animal, and good taste has brought women, not only to admire dogs of race, but to own and breed them and to contend for recognition as successful breeders at exhibitions all over the country.

These women are not of the "Brush, comb and bandoline" class that predominates around the cages of the wretched "toy" or "freak" dogs at exhibitions. They belong, as a rule, to the brightest, best cultured

I

and noblest girls and women in the country and their interest in dogs is not a "fad," but earnest and to last.

Evidence of this may be had by comparing the catalogues of the first bench shows with those of the present time. When fifteen years ago Miss Penniman, Miss Bessie R. Webb, Miss M. D. Wagstaff, Mrs. R. A. McCurdy and Miss E. T. Pratt, of New York, had the courage to place their favorites on exhibition, they felt a little abashed when they saw their names in the catalogue and in the newspapers. Now women whose names figure in reports of society gatherings, meetings to further humanitarian aims and educational schemes and as patronesses of art, music and drama, vie with men of their rank in exhibiting what they can do in dog-raising. It is no exaggeration to say that this is evolution and the test of the feeling of to-day and of 1877 is well illustrated by one fact. When the Rev. J. Cumming Macdona, of Cheadle rectory in Cheshire, England, one of the Queen's chaplains, came here in 1877 to exhibit the champion Irish setter, "Rover," and to judge four classes of dogs at the first bench show of the Westminster Kennel Club, all sorts of paragraphs and comments appeared in the newspapers and the general verdict was that he was a sporting parson and one of the Prince of Wales's "set." That year the entries numbered 1191 and there were many exhibits that would not pass muster to-day. This year there were 1375 entries and few of the animals were inferior exhibits.

YOUR DOG MUST FIT YOUR HOME.

As you should cut your coat according to your cloth, so should one choose a dog. How do you live ? Have you a room as your home, a flat, a house in a crowded neighborhood, one in a quiet street, or a suburban residence ? Have you a yard or a flat roof where you can exercise a dog or stables ? Do you own a carriage so that you can take your pet out for an airing and turn it on the road where it will annoy none and not be voted a nuisance or a dangerous animal by "canophobists"? Your dog must fit your house. In the country all things are possible in this way ; only you must look out for the prejudiced and the envious and their strychnine and arsenic. A St. Bernard would be just as much out of place in a bandbox flat in a city as an Alderney bull, and a delicate Blenheim spaniel would hardly care to rough it in the back woods.

POOR MEN'S DOGS HERE AND IN ENG-
LAND.

In all the large towns in England, and notably London, Manchester and Liverpool, the poorest artisan or clerk can—and generally does—possess a dog, and takes such care to get one of pure race that the pet is often a source of income, not only because its progeny are valuable, even when just weaned, but also because its owner invariably puts the animal in competition for prizes, not often at bench shows, but usually at gatherings of dog fanciers who go to them with their favorites under their arms. These contests are often in liquor saloons or rather in the rooms adjoining the bar, and of course there is much drinking over the event. The dogs exhibited, are, as a rule, fighters, "varmint" killers and "toys," but often men who live by their day's labor exhibit dogs of race that are as fine and pure as those shown at the grand exhibitions.

AN OBJECTIONABLE DOG ORDINANCE SYSTEM.

A BAR to such a custom in a great city like New York is the reckless, inadequate and absurd dog ordinance, which is protection that does not protect. Its enforcement is in the hands of ruffianly, blackmailing "Thugs," who have no respect for a license tag or a leading chain or for a delicate woman or child. They commit outrages every week, in the name of the law, because—to make their calling pay—they must in one way or another snatch up so many animals at thirty cents a head. The ordinance was due to the love of the poor man for the dog, and an ignorance of the evil of harboring mongrels, and the advantage of keeping nothing but animals of distinct race. These poor mongrels multiplied until they overran the streets and the popular-fallacy cry of hydrophobia brought about the passage of the ordinance. Now the mongrels are scarce, and the "hoodlums" who are licensed to enforce the law, prey on the well bred animal.

A better law would be one imposing a high dog-tax,

and this strictly enforced or the scattering of poisoned meat to the homeless curs, would protect dogs worth keeping and do away with animals that are really nuisances. When America attains to "a higher civilization," women and children will be safe from molestation when promenading with their pets, and there will be a place set apart in Central Park where there is a grass range and water for dogs to run unchallenged. With this boon may come the doing away of the prejudice which excludes dogs from public conveyances.

BEWARE OF MONGRELS AS PETS.

No one would plant weeds in a window box or a flower garden. Why have mongrels as pets? "Beware the mongrel," is a good rule for dog lovers. Another is, "Beware the puppy" and the friend who gives you a dog. If you buy a puppy, it is an act of faith, unless your purchase is made on a guarantee of unblemished race from a dealer of undoubted honesty. It is nice to wean and raise your own dogs, but an animal that is a year old has the advantage of having passed the period in which it is both a nuisance, by reason of inherent mischief loving and dirty tendencies, and also the age at which many dogs succumb to various ailments. When a dog is a year old, many of its race characteristics are plain and it learns to love and obey just as quickly as a puppy. Of course, if you own adult animals, you are sure of the purity of their progeny and the risk of being cheated does not exist. The animals so brought up are doubly valuable.

CLASSES OF DOGS OF RACE.

" Ay, in the catalogue ye go for men
As hounds and greyhounds, mongrels, spaniels, curs
Shoughs, water-rags and demi-wolves are 'clept
All by the name of dogs : the valued file
Distinguishes the swift, the slow, the subtle,
The housekeeper, the hunter ; every one
According to the gift which bounteous nature
Hath in him closed.—"

" Macbeth."

IF we take the breeds of dogs which are worth caring for and making friends of, because they are of distinct race and reproduce their kind and because they are fitted for this climate, they can be divided into the following classes :

Large and Field-sport dogs, the majority requiring grooming, water and a range.

First : Field-sport dogs ; setters of the various breeds, such as Irish, English, Gordons, Laveracks and Llewellyns.

Pointers of the heavy and light classes (over and under 55 pounds).

8

Hounds, including Staghounds, Bloodhounds, Fox-hounds, Harriers and Beagles.

Greyhounds, including Deerhounds.

Spaniels, including Irish, Water, Clumbers and large Cockers (Springers).

Retrievers, including Chesapeake-Bay dogs.

Second : Show or watch dogs, Great Danes, Mastiffs, St. Bernards, rough and smooth-coated, Newfoundlands, Russian Wolfhounds.

Small, or rather, house or—still better—home dogs.

First : Field sport dogs; Spaniels, small Cockers of both liver and white and black varieties and Dachshundes.

Second : Non-sporting; Fox-Terriers, rough and smooth-coated, Bedlingtons, Black and Tan, Bull-Terriers, Yorkshire s, Dandie Dinmonts, Irish-Terriers, Scotch-Terriers, Skye-Terriers, Collies, Italian greyhounds, Poodles, Pugs and Lap Spaniels, including Japanese, Blenheim and King Charles.

It will be observed that the above list does not contain the names of some races that are known, such as Esquimaux, Spitz, Coach-dogs, etc. This last breed was never fit to be the pet of any one but a stable man. It is simply a show dog possessed of a cross disposition, but handsomely marked and the continuation of a " fad " that made it an appanage of a rich man's establishment. The other dogs could be tolerated if they could annually meet the fate of " L'homme à l'oreille cassée " from May to October. They are Arctic creatures to whom life is only worth living with the thermometer at from 65 degrees to where alcohol freezes, creatures of the snow and ice floe who are miserable in warm weather.

DOGS THAT ARE FITTED FOR CITY LIFE.

WE all have more or less the sporting instinct and it is, of course, pleasant to own a dog that may be at the same time a companion and a guardian, and also a friend in the field. It is very hard, however, in cramped quarters to properly keep one of the large sporting dogs. It is all right as long as the shooting season lasts. As soon as it is over, the dog returns in fine condition to its home to be petted, overfed, and spoiled. Instead of hunting birds, and keeping "in form", it hunts slippers, plays with the babies and becomes aldermanic from eating between meals. A pointer or a setter may very easily be kept in a house if feeding promiscuously can be prohibited, and if it can be given a wide range every day.

The pointer, by the way, does not suffer so much from absence from water as the setter, and for this reason prairie chicken shooting is almost always over pointers. They can be watered from a keg and only need water every half-hour. With the setter it is different. Its comfort, almost its existence, depends

on its having free access to water while in the field,
and no setter summers well and is fit for the field
in the fall, unless it has been taken to water where
it can bathe at least once a week. Of course, even in
a flat, it could be soused in the bath tub, but there is a
line to be drawn somewhere, and most women draw it
at dogs using the place where they bathe.

Still, as has been said, it is possible to keep a setter
or a pointer in close quarters in New York, provided
always that the animal has a run twice a day. Ten
times a day would be better. A yard or a flat roof
helps matters wonderfully.

Of the hounds, the Dachshunde and Beagle are more
easily kept in close quarters than their larger brethren,
but they must have exercise and must not be pam-
pered. It is almost impossible to keep a Greyhound
or a Deerhound in a large city. Their life is in their
speed. They must have exercise to live. Not so the
spaniels. Nearly all of them make admirable home
dogs, even the Irish and the Clumbers. Retrievers and
Chesapeake dogs are not house dogs.

The man who wishes to keep a Great Dane, a
Mastiff, a St. Bernard, a Newfoundland or a Russian
Wolfhound should have special quarters for it. The
best home for one of these immense animals is a
stable or an outhouse, and it is hardly possible to
keep one in good condition without employing an
attendant to minister to its wants and to give it its air-
ings. Even then, in a great city, the animal would

suffer. It would have to be promenaded on a chain, or let loose, so muzzled as to render it miserable. Large dogs are not fitted for large cities. They may be ornaments, but they become spirit-broken unless they have freedom, exercise and access to water.

Of the smaller dogs several are specially fitted for city life and thrive though " cribbed, cabined and confined. " The best ? Well, this is, naturally, a matter of choice. Some choose one breed, some another, but the all-round, home dog for a large city is a terrier whose coat shall be neither woolly nor silky.

THE GIANT PETS OF RACE.

" 'Tis sweet to hear the watch dog's bark,
Bay deep-mouthed welcome as we draw near home."

Byron.

THE great show or watch dogs referred to, Danes,
formerly known as Siberian or Ulm dogs, Mastiffs,
St. Bernards, Newfoundlands and Russian Wolfhounds are more ornamental than useful, if we may
except what they may do as watch dogs and, in the
case of the Newfoundland, the possibility that it might
save a life from drowning. All are fitted for the country ; none flourish unless they have large, airy quarters,
constant exercise and some access to water. The
Danes and Mastiffs, when their savage instincts are
developed, are dangerous and ferocious beasts, not to
say man eaters.

Indeed the Dane, when kept by a German, is not
regarded as fit for watch service or as a body guard,
unless trained " on the man. " It is taught that the
throat of a marauder or its master's enemy is the
target for its teeth and there are special professors in
large cities who instruct this race in the art of spring-

ing at the most vulnerable part of a biped oppo-
nent.

It is in the blood of the animal to do this. It did
it in the days of ancient Rome, for if one race of dogs
has preserved its characteristics as to form, as depicted
in sculpture and sketches which antedate the Christian
era, it is this haughty, fierce-looking animal, which is
not always to be depended upon even by its master,
especially if it has come into his possession when adult.
Well trained, it is the best of big watch dogs and a
picturesque addition to a country establishment.

The Mastiff, too, is not of modern creation. A
century ago noblemen in England came to be jealous
of their Mastiff kennels and to hoard their stock.
Cast iron restrictions were put on their servants and
dependants so as to prevent a single animal capable of
reproducing the strain from leaving the kennels. If
one was given away, it was either a female, not gravid,
or an emasculated dog. The race was bred "in and
in" without heed of the perils of consanguinity and
the result was the preservation of the strain, so that it
was kept as pure as that of the Godolphin Arabian, but
the animals ran down in form and to jaw malformation.

A quarter of a century ago the absolute necessity of
new blood in the race to · prevent utter deterioration,
compelled those who owned the best stock in the
world to introduce strange sires and dams into their
kennels and to sell or give their dogs to others equally
in want of new blood. Among other kennels thus

broken up was that of Baron Grantley of Bramley
in Surrey, which had held animals that the Sovereign
could not have at a king's ransom. So the breed
rapidly improved and the result was that in 1887 Mr.
A. A. Brown sent here the famous " Norma," " Mable "
and " Saxon II." to snatch honors from dogs that had
not been reared under patrician auspices.   The Mastiff, with its negro-black head, fawn colored, supple
body, and magnificent frame, inspires as much respect
as admiration. As a rule, it is docile to its master and
safe with women and children, but when old and cross
it is dangerous and when its ferocity is aroused, it is
Satan unchained.

The St. Bernard of both species, the rough and
smooth-coated, can, in this country, serve little other
purpose than that of ornament. It is a magnificent
beast, if it receives more care in the matter of grooming and exercise than a blooded horse of high price
needs, and one or two of them "set off" a lawn or a
porch admirably, and they form a noble escort to a
village cart. As watch dogs, however, their usefulness
lies in their deterrent rather than their aggressive
value. The most hardened of tramps would hesitate
before passing a canine sentinel with a head like a
lion's and a body as large as that of a calf. As to
choice between the rough and smooth-coated, only this
is to be said : The dog with the least coat suffers the
least in warm weather. The new acquisition, Sir Bed-
ivere, valued at $25,000, was almost in a state of col-

lapse at the last New York Bench Show, although the thermometer marked but a little over 70.

Have we any Newfoundlands here? Very few, if the correct type is to be accepted as a criterion of value. The exhibitions recently have been wretched, while in England they have been very good. It is a faithful, docile and intelligent beast, indispensable where there are children who disregard maternal advice and "go near the water," provided it has had a few lessons, first in recovering articles thrown in the water, and then in rescuing a child able to swim but who will simulate one in peril.

No dog has suffered so much from the tricks of dog "jockeys" to satisfy an incorrect public standard of excellence as the Newfoundland. The race came of crossing, but the proper type is a jet black animal; white breasts are not blemishes by any means, and its coat should have a little wave in it, but this should not by any means tend so much to curliness as to be what, among women, is known as "good-natured hair." The popular fallacy was that the dog should be huge, with a coat as kinky as an Ethiopian's wool, and the dealers, by crossing, supplied the demand, until what appeared to be uninteresting runts took the prizes at the shows and enlightened the victims of the "jockeys."

The Russian Wolfhounds are new to us. They used to appear in the "miscellaneous" class. They appear to be a distinct race, so far as the Greyhound type of them is concerned. Another type of them is a mongrel one. They are fleet and courageous and are said to be good watch dogs. They are certainly graceful, so much so as to suggest the inquiry, "Could they cope with the wolf?"

The choice of any of the dogs named in the list of field sport dogs must be determined by the taste and purses of those who select them, the sport that is to be had and the accommodations the animals can be given.

What has been said about long and short coated dogs applies to them, if we may except the Spaniels, which, with proper care and exercise, and occasional access to water, flourish even in such cramped quarters as a city flat, while they are glorious fellows at a country home.

Pointers and Setters of all the strains must be bought on pedigree and guarantee, and a safe guide is the American Kennel Club Stud Book, which records pedigrees and is largely to be trusted as a guarantor of race. This treatise cannot discuss the value of the various strains of these breeds, but it may venture to say that in nine cases out of ten, the light-colored dog is more valuable in the woods than the dark one, because it can the easier be seen, but such a dog in the city shows uncleanliness of coat more markedly than one of darker color. Pointers are more often snappish than Setters, and are, therefore, more undesirable for playmates, unless their temper has been thoroughly tested.

The big hounds are not home dogs, and are as much out of place in the city as Greyhounds, unless the owner has extraordinary and unexceptionable facilities for keeping and exercising them. And here appears to be the place to say that the keeping of dogs in "hutch" kennels in the open air, which is injurious to any breed anywhere, is an infamy in a city, and outrageous when the "hutch" is in a yard on which the sun never shines. Silvio Pellico's "Prigioni" were palaces to such dank, cheerless, temper-wrecking cells. Better to trust to your friends or hire a dog when the shooting season begins, than to spoil the traits of your field companion and court rheumatism and other ailments by such imprisonment.

The Dachshunde, however, which is not only a rabbit dog of merit, but when properly trained a valuable aid in deer tracking, can be kept without much trouble or risk in a city. It is one of the most docile of the dog family and when of pure strain almost priceless. It's a queer little fellow with a keen, sharp, inquisitive head, a kid glove coat and bandy legs that are as monstrously ugly as its head and trunk are lovely. The Beagle, a rabbit hound, dwarf brother to the Harrier, Fox and Staghound, might also be kept in cramped town quarters. But neither it nor our bandy-legged friend is, as a rule, a good watch dog, but they get along well with the little folks.

A little enthusiasm about the Spaniels is pardonable. They are to-day what they were 400 years ago—

blue-blooded by reason of remote ancestry and unsul-
lied lineage. The Irish and Water Spaniels even
can be kept in a flat if given enough exercise and a
run to water occasionally and all of them are deli-
ciously cute ; born trick dogs, excellent field dogs and
good guardians and playmates. As dogs for hunting,
their methods differ from those of the pointer and
setter as, unless specially trained, they do not stop
when game is discovered but rout it up and announce
its presence by barking. The forte of the Cockers
and Clumbers is woodcock and ruffed grouse ; the
others are all round dogs for game and water fowl.
Few are quail dogs.

The most admirable and the largest of the spaniel
family is the Clumber, a delightful, lumbering, short-
legged fellow, with an orange and white coat, each
hair of which is like spun glass. It has not found
favor enough in this country to be launched as a caprice of fashion, simply because in the whole of the
United States and in Canada there are not twenty
couples of pure bred animals. It makes as good a
house dog under favorable circumstances as it is a
keen and admirable field dog.

As has been said elsewhere, the Retriever, a dog of
uncertain lineage, useful to pick up dead or wounded
game, and the Duck or Chesapeake Bay dog are not
house dogs for a city.

OUR HOME DOG.

" The little dogs and all."

King Lear.

THIS chapter deals with the terriers, Collies, the non-sporting Greyhounds, Poodles, Pugs and chamber spaniels. It will not deal with " Toy " or " Freak " dogs in the sense of speaking of them as desirable pets, for these reasons :—There is a market for everything that is grotesque, deformed, stunted or unnatural. Collections of such monstrosities are made and can be seen for a dime. The Japanese are clever in producing dwarfed deformities of trees because there is a market for such adornments. There was, and still is to a limited extent, a market for " Freak " or " Toy " dogs and the demand resulted in the furnishing of a supply of rickety, wretched, shivering abominations, principally in the Bull terrier, Yorkshire terrier and Black and Tan breeds. The dwarfing in case of the Bull and Black and Tan terriers is attained by choosing undersized sires and dams ; picking out the runts of their.progeny and physicking them from puppyhood to maturity. The Yorkshires, vile long-haired

and silky-polled dogs, came of crossing with the Scotch,
Skye, and Black and Tan breeds, to obtain form, color,
coat and sprightliness, and supply the demand for little
brutes that are seen in upholstered cages and attended
by women at every dog show.   Few of them reproduce
their kind.   In many cases maternity is fatal and
should a litter of—say Bull or Black and Tan—terrier toys be raised, luck alone furnishes a small whelp;
the others are nondescripts.

In the case of the Yorkshires, one litter out of three
furnishes a puppy that may some day be shown and
combed to a degree that is exasperating and its poll
pomaded and bandolined to make it appear attractive.   One romp or a failure to " fix it up " destroys the
illusion.   It becomes a blurred caricature of all the
races that have entered into its composition.   Its off-
spring are invariably sold at cheap rates as Scotch or
Skye terriers.   Shun " Toys " and " Yorkshires."

Few persons know what a keen, sprightly and ex-
quisitely shaped animal a Black and Tan terrier of the
" London type " is.   It is not the shivering, blue-
skinned, hair-denuded little wretch that among women
of no uncertain class commands such a high price.
It is a defiant, symmetrical, well-poised and game-to-
the-backbone home dog ; black as jet except where
the test of absolutely pure blood demands rich tan
markings.   Its limbs are fine, yet strong, its tail is
straight and shapely and the contour of its neck and
head are as correct as that of a race horse.   Few

home dogs are equally desirable in point of watchfulness, pluck, fidelity and gentleness.

And the Bull Terrier, what a difference between a "jockeyed" strain with a snubbed or short or dull, thick nose and the nervous, lithe, hard, yet short coated thoroughbred, dazzling-white where there is hair, rose-hued where nature provides no coat, and black nosed. What a keen head; what a quicksilver temperament; tail straight, but a little longer than the fine nose.

A Bull Terrier is born pugnacious and is a terrible fighter because of the structure of its jaws, which have a punishing power due to their ability to open, alligator or snake fashion, far back. Yet, if properly raised, it can be depended on as the most faithful and redoubtable of watch dogs and it may be trained to be as gentle with women and children as any other. It, like the true Black and Tan, can be kept in any city home.

An equally desirable house dog is the Cocker spaniel of both the liver, liver and white and black varieties, if at least once a year it has an outing in the country and can occasionally be taken to give free vent to its exuberant spirits, where it can range and indulge in the luxury of a bath. It is unsurpassed as a pet if it be not old or ailing; is as handsome a parlor ornament as a Persian cat, is a famous watch dog and learns to be cunning in tricks quicker than any dog, except, perhaps, a poodle. Apart from this, it is an intelligent and useful com-

panion in the country, especially when its master wants
an hour or so of recreation in a woodcock cover, if he
will only have patience, keep it in sight and be ever
alert to have the range any "longbill" may take when
starting. But buy no Cocker unless on guarantee and
keep no animal that is long-legged or without ears,
feathered almost to the ground and well marked. The
limit for weight for a liver and white Cocker is fifteen
pounds. The best for home dogs are between eleven
and thirteen pounds. As to markings, choose an animal well ticked over the fore legs and nose, in prefer-
ence to one having uniform patches of color. The
progeny of ill marked dogs are less well marked than
they invariably, and this deterioration in beauty of
marking is progressive by generation.

The Poodle is essentially a house dog, be it Russian
or French. The animal in characteristics is a household imp, not averse to mischief or brawling. When
once started it is a desperate fighter, but it rarely attacks
mankind and is a good watch dog. Fashion has made
it grotesque and indecently so, but those who keep such
shorn beasts have the courage of their convictions.

A house dog to which the heart warms by reason of
romantic and literary associations is the Collie, the
most gentle, constant and lovable of any race. Sym-
pathetic and unobtrusive in its instincts and quaintly
human in its traits, unless perverted by example or en-
couragement, it lacks dog nature so far as hunting tendencies and the worrying of such "small deer" as cats,

rats and mice are concerned ; but it can be trusted as well by the cradle as in the sheep-fold, and although happier and healthier in a free range, it adapts itself easily to city life. No dog so soon learns the ways of a household or is so slow to forget those who have cared for it.

Our friend, the Pug, was cast in a more stolid and philosophical and less sentimental mould, but really fine bred ones of the Willoughby or Morrison strain are rarely to be had at prices within the reach of any but the rich. It is a desirable home pet because it is clean-coated, docile and odorless. It is, however, a miserable guardian, stolid as a burgher and as a rule undemonstrative.

The Fox Terrier, while as clean-coated as the Pug, is as demonstrative and mercurial as the other is phlegmatic and quiet-loving. It is impossible to name a better dog for a city home, be it cramped or spacious. It is a self-assertive little fellow, not prone however to quarrel, but ever active in search of experiences, the gratification of curiosity or in search of such mild distractions as cat chasing and rat killing. It is " all dog ", to use the experience of an enthusiast, and in that term is comprehended its faults ; it would be a little too lively in a staid household. As a watch dog, it is the peer of any and is rarely cross with children. The rough coated variety is even more hardy than the short coated one, but he is objected to on the ground that the contrast between them is as great as between a spruce young dandy and an unshaven proletarian.

Of the rough-coated terriers, whole chapters might be written on each. All are admirable as guardians, companions, and "varmint killers." A choice among them must depend upon personal taste. The best, probably, would be the Irish-Terrier, because it is the least masked by hair, and its game head is exceedingly taking. It is possibly of all house dogs the one that has the wiriest coat, each individual hair being almost as coarse as a bristle. Its coat is a charming filbert brown in hue and its pluck is indomitable.

A Dandie Dinmont is another cute fellow with two heavy coats; one a coarse outside, one of pepper and salt, mustard, flint or belton shade, with an inner one; a soft, silky pile and a scimetar tail. It has all the characteristics which make an Irish-Terrier attractive.

So few real Skye-Terriers exist that the true animal is almost unknown. Anything that is long and hairy with a fuzzy face is called a Skye. The dog of race, however, is an animal at least three times as long as it is high at the shoulders. It has a coat as coarse as horse hair and so long that, parted on the back, it could almost trail on the ground; it is short-legged, and shock headed with long, expressive ears carried jauntily and a peculiar trundling gait. Its colors are steel-gray, blue, pepper and salt, and black. The Bedlington terrier is of the same form, but its coat has a tendency to kink and be woolly.

The Scotch-Terrier is much like the Irish, only its color should be a rich cream or fawn or rufous, and the texture of the coat should run from wiry and short on the back to a little less harsh and lighter in hue on the head. A Scotch-Terrier should never be blue. Those that are sold as such are the useless progeny of the so-called Yorkshire or they are nondescripts.

The lap dogs comprise the delicate Italian Greyhound and the King Charles, Blenheim, and Japanese Spaniels; all of them date back to the 16th century. They are useless as watch dogs but singularly ornamental. The Greyhounds are exotics and in cold weather are wretched, chilly little things, but in fine weather they romp like other dogs and are as graceful as gazelles. The have not been in fashion for years, more's the pity. Blenheims and King Charles spaniels have been fashionable for three centuries and were never so cheap as to be within the reach of persons whose means are moderate. Like the Mastiffs and some other breeds they, half a century ago, could be found of pure pedigree only with persons of rank or fortune who were so selfish as to refuse either to sell them or give them away and the result was "in-breeding" and deterioration.

To-day it would be difficult to find either a Blenheim or King Charles with a perfectly even jaw. All are more or less "undershot" or "overshot," as the projection of the under or upper jaw is termed. A lovelier pet than a thoroughbred orange and white Blenheim spaniel is not to be found, and no dog is handsomer than a glossy, black King Charles with rich tan markings. But the sums asked for even second class dogs are exorbitant. A fine Blenheim would be cheap at $500 and $350 is usually asked for a King Charles. Their pedigrees should date to Nell Gwyn. The little leggy and ill-feathered Japanese spaniel is a pretty, innocent little dog that has had little success in America. None of these lap dogs have any merit as guardians. Were they to face a maurauder and could speak they would probably say, with the coon, "Is that you, Cap'n? I'll come down."

The Bull Dog has not been described because it cannot be regarded as a safe pet or a desirable watch dog. If because of its cynical ferocity and unpreposessing traits, both of face and structure, it is regarded as an acquisition, that may explain why some prefer it to other breeds and it does explain why it should not be recommended as a home dog. Other dogs are not spoken of because they have hitherto been in the "miscellaneous" class and may be looked upon if not with suspicion, as pertaining to the class nondescript.

THE CHOICE AND COST OF A DOG.

THE preceding chapters have flashed some caution signals, and discussed dogs in relation to their adaptability to our climate and the breeds suitable for confined quarters as well as more spacious houses, mansions and the country, and they have praised some breeds as adapted for close city keeping, and as valuable for distinct race characteristics. The reader who intends to own a dog has doubtless at least an idea of the kind of animal that would suit his tastes and home. If not, he should study the subject and decide. Such study can be made at exhibitions of dogs, or by looking at pure blooded animals belonging to others, but as has been said before, "Beware of the mongrel and the dog that comes to you without unquestioned guarantee."

It will be just as unpleasant to devote a year to the development of a dog only to find that it would have no chance of notice in an exhibition, as it would be pleasant, and should be possible, to raise one and see a judge at a bench show put the blue ribbon of first honor on its collar. Nothing in dogs is worth harboring unless it is first class in every respect. No smattering of dog lore will enable an amateur to cope with reckless or untrustworthy dealers. On the other hand it does no harm, and is a pleasant recreation, to learn as much as possible about dogs of the house. Knowledge of them comes intuitively, and if interest in them is pushed to the verge of a " fad," so much the better. It will arm the student against imposition, provided he select one or two breeds and devote his whole attention to them.

If for instance, the student should choose as his home pet an Irish-Terrier, or a Cocker Spaniel, not only the literature devoted to them would be interesting to him, but he would have a live interest in those owned by others, in exhibitions, and in the chat about them in the publications which make a specialty of dog lore.   Such publications are legion, and a few of them are trustworthy, interesting, and not vehicles for the schemes of irresponsible and unscrupulous " jockeys."

This work cannot undertake to recommend any such publications.   Selections can be made by getting sample numbers from a news dealer, and individual judgment and tastes will dictate the choice.

In deciding upon the breed of dog that he wishes, a purchaser would do well to decide leisurely; first as to characteristics that please, and secondly as to what animal would suit his house. As a rule, financial considerations should not weigh in the matter. If a puppy is chosen, it is simply investing in a lottery. In such cases, assuming that the puppy be less than two months old, the rarest and choicest strains seldom command more than $50, while the usual price for such a canine baby is from $10 to $15. With a guarantee, any one who thinks such a sum large for a dog should either await a present of a puppy, or abandon the idea of possessing one of blue blood.

With this outlay he has to suffer much annoyance. Young dogs are as fractious, as unpleasant in habits, and as subject to fatal ailments as babies, but the dog raised, it is treasured more than one that is acquired when adult. It is impossible to name a sum for a dog of any breed one year old, and therefore past the period of great risks, tutored in clean ways and weaned of mischievousness. The amount must be determined by the purse of the buyer, the intensity of his purpose to own a dog, the strain of the animal and the reasons which prompt the owner to sell. While a good liver and white Cocker Spaniel, a capital Fox-Terrier, and an entirely unobjectionable Black and Tan-Terrier of the strict, large type should command from $50 to $100, an entirely reasonable sum, fabulous amounts might be asked for some animals of these breeds simply because some very rich persons are willing and able to pay them. A fine and absolutely perfect Pug, a Collie of rare strain, an Irish or Skye-Terrier, a Bull-Terrier of the true type, is worth just what its owner will sell it for. Dachshundes of patrician blood and perfect Blenheim and King Charles Spaniels, like the large dogs, St. Bernard's Mastiffs, and Great Danes, always command fancy prices as do rare orchids, violins or books, but cost, so far as such dogs are concerned, is hardly a criterion of really intrinsic value. As a rule, $15 for a puppy, and $75 for a dog or gyp one year old are prices that are reasonable.

HAVING CHOSEN THE DOG.

HAVING chosen the dog that is to be your home friend, from among the kinds named, and on the suggestions given, it is assumed that you have one of distinct race, capable of reproducing its kind and not likely to be the parent of mongrels, if mated to one equally pure-blooded. You have, it is also assumed, disregarded new "fads," and "created" breeds from the miscellaneous classes, such as Schipperkes Whippets, Welsh, White English, and so on, and have steered clear of the shoals and rocks on which many an enthusiast has been wrecked, in admiration for animals that are fluffy, woolly, or silky in coat and "so cunning," like the Yorkshire Terrier, or the dwarfs and unhappy "Toys," or the hairless freaks of China and Mexico. Your task now is to make your dog and your home mutually suitable.

3

INSTALLATION OF THE PET.

IF your acquisition is a puppy, it has to pass a period of probation, the duration of which depends on the amount of liberty it gets in some place where it cannot be a nuisance, the intelligence of its mentor and corrector, and its appreciation of what are the ethics of polite society, and the nature of its reproofs or chastisements. It is impossible to lay down rules for the training of a puppy, so that it may learn that correction awaits it if it is unclean in clean places, noisy where quiet reigns, or mischievous. Be the dog little or small, a revolver is better than a stick, or even a cane. The best trained dog is one that appreciates a vocal reproof.

First, assign quarters to the pet, be it large or small. If a baby dog, some out-of-the-way place in a box, out of which it cannot crawl, should be devoted to it. A hall, a recess, or a lumber room will do. A cellar is the worst place, an airy loft the best. Let it appreciate that where it sleeps is its headquarters. An adult dog takes more kindly to a new billet than a young one, but it should have a different bed. The

34

best for an adult is a remnant of carpet sufficiently large for its comfort, attached to the floor so that it cannot be scratched up. A puppy should sleep on an old woollen garment that can be washed frequently or replaced.

It is better in close quarters for an adult to have a screw eye bolt arranged in its sleeping place, so that at stated hours it can be chained up for sleep at night, and released at a certain hour for exercise in the morning. During the day, it should have as much liberty as the apartment will permit. The chain and eye bolt can be otherwise utilized as a correctional measure, when there is ill-doing and marked disapproval becomes necessary, because reproof and mild correction have not been heeded. A dog should never be thrashed. As a rule, the voice should be as potent as a cuff, and if corporal punishment must be resorted to, the best instrument is a newspaper tightly folded in a roll like a club. A more severe chastisement can be administered with a large paper-covered book, and a slipper ought to inflict the severest thrashing that a house dog should be subjected to.

The blows should be given while the culprit is held by the nape of the neck, and freely distributed over the cheeks, forepaws and thighs, but the ears, mouth, abdomen and back should be spared. The thrashing should be accompanied by chidings, and it may be emphasized by other punishment, such as locking up,

deprivation of food, or an affectation of contempt at
its conduct.

The dispositions of dogs vary. The safest rule is,
after a correction, to chain the animal up or sequester
it and allow no one to go near it. This is a bar to the
animal seeking sympathy from others, or hiding away
or sulking. After awhile the corrector should visit the
animal and make peace with it, talking to it soberly
and sparing caresses, but no correction, vocal or phys-
ical, should be meted out unless the culprit is caught
red-handed, as it were, in noise, mischief or nastiness,
as it should understand precisely why it is punished.
Brutal chastisement is as absurd as it is useless and
cruel.

The writer once bought an admirable Irish Setter
that had passed several unhappy years with a brute
who was a fiend incarnate when angry, and to whom,
when correction was necessary or unnecessary, nothing
came amiss. Boots, fists, a gun barrel, or a fence rail
suited him equally well, and the dog was often laid up
by maimings. It soon learned to appreciate humane
treatment, and all that it needed was vocal remon-
strance and now and then a shake by the neck; it
would whine piteously for clemency if a few grass
stalks were gathered and shaken at it while its master
held it by the ear, the neck or a front paw. Sometimes rebel natures are discovered, and a dark cell and
bread and water correction have to be resorted to until
the animal surrenders and crawls up to lick the mas-

ter's hand. Any attempt at retaliation by biting should be punished instantly by a slipper thrashing and solitary confinement without food. Incorrigible offenders in this respect should be got rid of.

The home dog soon fraternizes with the domestic cat. The introduction will always be risky, and accompanied by zeal on the part of the one to put the other through its paces, and scurrying and spitting and tail elephantiasis, but, unless the cat has kittens, a truce is soon patched up and in time they will eat out of the same dish,—unless some stupid person "sics" the dog on the cat and encourages it to chase or worry it. Much of the tact necessary with young children tells wonderfully if applied to dog raising, and no animal detects more quickly injustice, caprice, neglect, or weakness. Let a dog learn that by acting "prettily" it may escape reproof or punishment, and it quickly becomes as detestable and as great a nuisance as a spoiled child.

THE DIETING OF A HOME DOG.

HERE are several golden rules :

1st. Never let your pet get accustomed to get even "snacks" while you are at meals.

2d. Let it have a set hour, rigidly observed for its meals.

3d. Never let it ask itself, "Have I an appetite?" If it turns up its nose at its food, withdraw the food. Wait five minutes, and if it exhibits the same contempt again, let it wait until the time for the next meal.

4th. Two repasts a day are sufficient for any dog.

5th. It is more humane to keep a dog so that it will be spare than to let it get obese, and then inflict an "anti-fat" régime.

6th. Be as particular with your pet's food as with your own, and let the vessels it uses be as clean always as the china on your table.

7th. Let it have access to pure, clean water in a proper vessel at all times of the day or night without its having to suffer or beg for it. A dog deprived of water for some time gulps it down when its craving is attended to, and its stomach and appetite suffer.

8th. Never give a dog raw meat, unless a veterinarian orders it.

To this may be added a protest against tin or any metal vessel. Earthenware or china is not too good for any dog. The drinking vessel, in which fresh water should be put at least three times a day, should be near the place assigned to the animal for sleeping, and if it be chained, it should be within easy reach of its chain. Such vessels should be at least five inches wide to prevent slopping when it laps and as heavy as possible, so that it may not easily be overturned and wet the dog's couch. Every time the water is changed, the vessel should be well rinsed. Good water is the life of a dog. It should not be too much trouble, when spring water cannot be had, to let water come to a boil, then bottle it and put it away where it will cool, but not in an ice box. As the dog needs it, pour it into the drinking vessel. Never let a dog drink milk that has not been boiled. It will have less risk of intestinal parasites and tubercular trouble.

Each dog's appetite varies, and some gain flesh more rapidly than others. The amount of food required for a pet can only be ascertained by observation. It must not gorge itself at any time. The safest way to test its appetite is to serve to it an ample dish of nourishment and watch it. If it is a glutton, it will gulp its food, and its aldermanic tendencies can only be checked by giving it rations in a couple of tablespoonfuls at a time. The amount necessary to sustain it can be judged by its conditions. When a dog's ribs cannot be well detected when it is active, it is too fat and its rations should be lowered.

Dogs that are not gluttons and in good health, generally eat heartily for a minute or so, hesitate, eat a little more, and appear to be disposed to allow the rest to remain for a lunch. Take what remains away. This hesitation comes of dog nature. It is an instinct of Providence. A dog with its freedom, on finding something to gorge on, generally carrion, will eat some and bury the rest. It simply provides for a rainy day, or as the French say, it is "*une poire pour la soif.*"

Do not attempt to raise your pet on milk, cereals and bread, nor believe that a dog does not need animal food. A dog to flourish should have a regimen as varied as a human being, but while it requires meat, and would hardly do without occasional bone nourishment, the basis of its food should be excellent corn and oatmeal, and clean and wholesome bread refuse. Disregard advice to feed your home dog on slops and "table refuse." If you do not and trust to "Bridget" fish, flesh, fowl, pastry, sweets and sauces will go to make an Olla Podrida for "Snap" which will soon entail a veterinarian's services.

A very good plan is to devote a deep frying pan or saucepan lined with enamel to the pet's cookery. Scrupulous cleanliness must be observed in its use, and in the selection of the food for the animal, which should be cooked once a day. The best time is in the afternoon, when it will be cooked and cooled in time for supper and the rest can be put away for breakfast. The most convenient hours for the dog's meals are 5 P. M. and 7 A. M. and it should have a good run after supper and before breakfast.

A nice way of getting up its food is to select some table scraps of meat from a joint of anything but pork, which have not been served with any sauce. Remove superfluous fat, but do not be too particular about this, and choose some cleanly cooked vegetables, such as boiled potatoes, cabbage, spinach or onions that have not had sauce of any kind on them. Stew the meat and vegetables for an hour and a half, turn the stew in a dish, and, taking the saucepan or the frying pan, put in it one, two, three or four spoonfuls of corn meal or oatmeal or corn and oatmeal mixed. Add enough water or the juice of the stew to prevent burning, and stir for a couple of minutes over the fire. Then turn in the stew. Incorporate the mixture and put it away to cool. The quantity of meal, etc., is regulated by the size, appetite and requirements of the dog. No such food should be kept longer than twenty-four hours. In less time it sometimes sours and should be rejected.

In serving the food, either pick out the lumps of meat or hide them under the food. Dogs are quaintly human, and treat meat in a stew as sailors raisins in "ornary" plum duff, or children molasses landscapes on bread and butter. They make sure of the most palatable of the dish, and eat the rest after. Such a stew should be sparingly seasoned with salt, never with pepper. Such a dish should be the dog's food five days of the week. It can be varied by lessening or increasing any of the ingredients. The other two days of the week, one can break the monotony of the regimen by giving milk that has been boiled and poured over broken crackers in the morning, and a beef rib or a mutton bone with some generous shreds of flesh on in the evening. This is the dogs tooth-brush. Now and then a chicken carcass without the leg and wing bones is good food, if the dog be mature, and have a full set of good teeth, but it is best to break the carcass with the flat of a hatchet, and to always watch for choking accidents.

Once a fortnight a dish of parboiled ox liver should be given as a meal. It is a great and grateful change and acts as a laxative. Another good meal which should replace the liver is a stew of ox or sheep's heart, but care should be taken to supply such meat food so that five meals of hash with ground cereals intervene, and in warm weather a dog should be humored into doing with as little animal nourishment as possible. The pets, in nine cases out of ten, will have to be starved into it, but they will not suffer if they reject three meals; they will eat the fourth under protest, but when the fifth is served they will be eager for it.

Puppies that are weaning, that is to say, not more than six weeks old, require nothing but first-class milk that has been brought to the boiling point, with the chill off, for two weeks, varied with pure buttermilk and now and then a piece of well-baked corn bread the size of a hickory nut, made palatable by soaking it for an instant in milk or meat soup. When they are two months old they may be taught to eat thicker nourishment, and a beef or mutton bone freed of spiculae and with a very little cooked meat on it makes them happy and helps along dentition. Care should be taken, however, to ascertain when the puppies serrated or milk teeth begin to get loose, so that it may not swallow them while eating.

Broth for ailing and weak dogs should be made by cutting up raw beef, mutton or chicken in small dice, putting the pieces in a wide-mouthed bottle, so that they will pack lightly by a shake. Fill the bottle to the top of the meat with cold water, and keep it in a vessel of boiling water for three hours or put the bottle in a jar filled with water to a level with the water in the bottle, and keep the jar in an oven, taking care to replenish the water in it to the level named for two hours; then let the bottle cool, and pass the contents through clean linen, taking care to squeeze the broth from the meat which is now useless animal fibre. Season the broth lightly with salt. If the animal's condition is not very serious, the broth can be given with wholesome bread refuse, corn, bread, crackers, or dog biscuits. At least once a month, examine you dog's mouth. If young and it has loose puppy teeth, extract them as soon as they can be moved to an angle of 45 degrees. If old, look out for loose or decayed teeth, and induce a dentist to operate on them. If they become covered with tartar get a dentist's instrument and remove it, taking care, however, not to injure the enamel. A last advice : feed your own dog yourself if you wish its friendship to be enduring.

ABLUTIONS.

ALL dogs in towns need bathing at least once a month. The animal's health and cleanliness depend largely on the condition of its coat. Short coated dogs require a slight soaping and a rinse ; long coated ones a careful wash and a removal of the soap in several changes of water. Warm, not hot water should be used. The best soaps are tar or sulphur or carbolic for long-coated animals, and castile soap for short-coated, such as Fox or Black and Tan terriers. Dip the dog in water, soap it, rinse it according to the length of its coat and its capacity to retain lather, and after it has been drained off on an old cloth and in a place free from draughts—this should not take more than a minute—wrap it in an old but clean sheet or blanket, and stow it away in a box or basket or in some place whence it cannot escape. It will soon be warm, and will gradually get dry enough to be released without fear of catching cold. When entirely dry, if it be a long coated dog, comb it with a coarse comb, unravelling any knots that may be in its coat, tail or ears, and brush it with a brush that would not be too

45

harsh for human hair. It will then shake itself into form and forget its martyrdom. In the country with free access to water and grass no dog needs a washing, but all the long coated ones should have a grooming occasionally, when the appearance of their coats warrants it.

CROPPING, DOCKING AND OTHER MUTILATIONS.

FASHION and tradition have decreed that certain dogs, such as black and tan terriers, shall be cropped or lose part of their ears, and that others, such as fox terriers, shall be docked or lose a portion of their tail. These mutilations make the animals smart looking, and in the case of the quarrelsome breeds the loss of part of the ear avoids laceration in disputes. Tail shortening, while a mutilation, can hardly be objected to, as the operation should be performed when the animal is but a few days old, and generally before it can see. It is an instantaneous one, and rarely excites a whimper. Ear cutting is a more cruel operation, as to be successful it should be done when the animal is well out of puppyhood, and the cutting is attended by loss of blood and much suffering, and the victim is an invalid for at least a week. In warm weather, such an operation should be prohibited.

47

MUZZLES, CHAINS AND HARNESS.

OUR home pets knew what harness and muzzles were in the time of Robbie Burns and Pope. Burns in his " Twa dogs " says :

> " His locked, lettered, braw brass collar,
> Showed him a gentleman and a scholar."

And Pope on the collar of the dog he gave to a friend had engraved :

> " Pray tell me, sir, whose dog are you ? "

Such gewgaws as collars and harnesses and muzzles have caused much suffering. Harnesses, such as are used for pug dogs, are simply a freak of fashion. Collars, chains and muzzles are needed, but if ill made, heavy, or too tight, they are instruments of torture and bring about deformities and ailments. No collar can be too soft or light, and no muzzle too loose so long as it fulfils the requirements of ordinances, prevents biting and is secure. Eye troubles, deafness, calloused necks, spinal and cerebral troubles, and numerous other ailments follow the use of heavy collars, while tight ones affect the throat and the respiration. The enormous and weighty neck gear on some of the larger dogs are cruel affairs, and some of the muzzles used, either pinch the jaws or hurt the neck. No muzzle should prevent a dog from using its voice or drinking, and no chain should be heavier than is absolutely necessary to hold the animal to its stall or place of rest. In leading a dog, a leather thong should always be used. It will not, as it is under surveillance, have an opportunity to gnaw it, and it is not made dejected and spiritless by the drag of weighty metal.

4

QUARTERS AND TRAINING FOR THE LARGER DOGS.

IF your pet be an animal used for hunting birds or furred game, by all means be liberal in its sporting education. Discover among your acquaintances those who hunt; be with them when they so do, and watch their dogs. If you find animals that instead of rioting in the field, disobeying, jumping in at the discharge of a gun, or being addicted to worrying game that has been killed or wounded, range systematically, are prompt in obedience, " down charge " when the gun speaks and mouth game tenderly, inform yourself as to the breaker, and take your dog to him.

Deer and rabbit hounds require training with dogs that have been blooded on the quarry they hunt, and 75 per cent of them turn out to be only second class as hunters. You can choose what style of training your dog shall have. Some breakers train to gesture, some to voice. Your bird dog may be taught to " down charge " when a gun is fired, or to stand until the order is given to " go on," or " dead bird." Some dogs are taught to retrieve game; others to simply point at it. The better dog is the one, staunch at gun fire, which simply indicates the game that has been killed or wounded.

In speaking of quarters, it is assumed that if you are in town you have a place where a kennel can be arranged for your dog, or if in the country, you have ground on which one can be built. The essentials in either case are airiness in a locality that is neither damp, bleak nor draughty, but light and comfortable, and above all, walls that will not harbor vermin, and a floor that will absorb no liquid that will taint. The site of such a place is readily found, and light and ventilation without draughts are not difficult to manage. If you have a large collection of dogs, say more than six, and keep them in your kennel at all seasons of the year, you must have arrangements for cool quarters in summer, and snug ones in winter.

Any good sporting journal not at the beck of dog fighters, or the freaks of "fanciers" will furnish plans for such a house, but, if you can afford it, spend all the money that is necessary to secure a main floor of cement, stone, pavement, zinc covered boards or flags, so that it can be flushed with water that should run to a gutter. The walls may be of brick, tiles, zinc over wood, or whitewashed wood over tarred paper. The intent of the waterproof floor is to avoid taint, and that of the walls to prevent the harboring of parasites. Vermin and bad odors ruin dogs' noses and tempers.

The dogs should have a board platform or benches

raised at least four inches from the floor, with ample
sleeping benches. The platforms and benches should
be set up so as to be readily removed for the thorough
cleaning of every inch of the main floor. Clean straw
is good bedding ; sawdust the most objectionable. Excellent bedding mats can be made of long straw with a
packing needle and twine.

They should not be too elaborate, not too closely
packed, nor cost much. Children can make them by
the gross if necessary. They should be half as long
again, and one and one half times as wide as the animal that is to sleep on them. They should be fastened
down by a cleat nailed at each end to prevent the animal raking them up. They should be burned when
unfit for further use. Coarse but very strong rag car-
pets, so made that they will support at least ten
thorough cleansings are more costly, but they have
this advantage, if vermin are present they are carried
away in them. The carpet that is to be cleaned
should be folded in the kennel, put in an old barrel,
and soaked with a 1,000 solution of bi-chloride of
mercury for twenty-four hours ; then treated to a bath,
wrung, soft soaped, rinsed until all the soap is gone,
and hung into the open air until thoroughly dried.

This is a winter couch for valuable large dogs, but it
should be nailed, battened, or cleated down to prevent
its being scratched up into a pillow. Three such rugs
should last the largest St. Bernard the whole winter.
The animal will attempt to scratch the rug up, of course,

but should be checked, and after a while it will take kindly to the couch which, if laid over straw that is clean, is neat and comfortable, and not too good for a good dog. All couches should be so arranged that the occupants can be excluded from them or kept on them, and each animal's sleeping quarters should be isolated, —that is to say, that, except in the case of puppies, only one dog should sleep on a couch and should not be within reach of another.

Yards to such kennels, if yards there must be, should be of pebbles, broken up, conglomerate or fine rock with sand or sandstone rammed hard over the foundation as compactly as possible, if the cost of cement or pavement is considered too great. But such yards should be dug out and re-made at least twice a year, as their materials absorb liquid solutions and become foul. A free range outside a kennel is preferable to any yard. No cesspool should be near any kennel, and no cooking should be done in any. Sick dogs have no place in them, if well dogs are there.

TRAINING THE HOME DOG.

CHARACTER is as varied in dogs as in human beings. In home pets are found the vivacious and the dull, the bold and the shy, the apt and the stupid, the kind and the cross. Generally a bond of sympathy and perfect understanding can be forged between the master and pet by careful observation and training. Force and harshness will always mar a dog. Intelligent treatment and the establishment of confidence, will, in the majority of cases, make one. The best rule to follow is the principles underlying the treatment of children.

As has been said before, a dog detects fraud and false principles as readily as does a child, and as readily becomes spoiled and incorrigible. The first lesson should be to come when called and remain where summoned until permission is given it to go. It should get a name at the start, and never be summoned except by name unless it be a field dog, trained to act on gestures or whistle. It is a bad plan to summon any other pet by a whistle or finger snapping. When it comes it should receive a caress, and sometimes, not often, a delicacy, such as a piece of bread. Never let it have sugar. It injures the teeth and impairs appetite.

Once drilled in this part of the manual, it should easily be taught to fetch and bring. Don't use a ball, if possible. One of large size stretches and hurts the mouth ; a small one of less than two inches in diameter invites accident. If a ball is used, it should be of tough leather, never a rubber ball. A good training toy can be made by a cobbler, either of sole leather four inches long, an inch and one quarter in diameter, or leather less thick over a piece of wood an inch in diameter, or of a wad of stiff paper the same size bound round with twine, but chide gnawing always, and let your aim be to train the dog so that it will be alert to see the toy and bring it quickly to you.

Make much of the dog as soon as it understands what you want. It will, if not extremely obtuse, soon learn the trick of holding the toy in its mouth, and to carry it if it has an intelligent mentor, quick to seize on its endeavors to obey and bend its dog sense to his wishes. Scolding does not help the pupil at all, and patience is the great secret of all training. The higher accomplishments, such as going away to seek slippers or hidden articles, can only be taught by earnest and intelligent labor, and the tuition must always be in the same groove. Commands to do this must always be given in the same tone and in the same words.

For instance, the trick of seeking hidden articles depends much on the dog's marvellous sense of smell.

The article hidden has its own odor ; so has the master's hand. The dog's attention is drawn to the article frequently, so as to familiarize it with its peculiarity and odor. In time it will become interested whenever it is produced. Hide it somewhere in the presence of the dog, making it a partner to the cache. At first it will endeavor then and there to take it away, but chide it, repeating the name of the article. Coax it away after a time, not speaking of the article. Go to another room, or if it be in the country, some distance off, and naming the article, say "fetch," or "get it," as you would do in the fetch and carry drill.

The dog may go back at once to the article and bring it, or it may look puzzled and bark at you, as if to say, " What on earth do you want ? " In this case walk back to the article exhibiting immense interest in it, and then repeat the going away and the demand to fetch. A few such lessons and the trick is learned.

The same patience and system are required for other feats. Sitting up, standing up, and even sitting down again are just as easily taught. The first lesson is given in the angle of a wall, and the dog is seated on its haunches, and put back in that position each time it endeavors to get on its four feet or lie down, and until it remains seated. Then it should be called away and made much of. By and by it will sit up and beg· A *bonne bouche* should be its reward. Later on when it begs it can be taught to rise on its hind legs by raising the coveted morsel and patience will result in its learning to turn in that position.

One of the hardest tricks after this is to get it to resume the sit-up or begging position. Somehow or another, dogs appear to suspect a practical joke in this trick, such as a crooked pin, and few ever learn to return to the sitting position other than in an undecided, gingerly fashion, and never smartly. The trick of following in the open air, instead of romping or running ahead, is one much more difficult, as it involves absolute obedience, and the curbing of the animal's jubilation over freedom and its curiosity.

AILMENTS AND NOSTRUMS.

WHEN you own a dog that you value, your first care should be to put yourself in touch with a veterinary surgeon, with a view of having his services in an emergency. Failing this, and an emergency arising, call on your family doctor. Canine pathology is in these days more or less familiar to every physician worthy of being consulted for human ailments or accidents. The adage, "A little knowledge is a dangerous thing," applies to dosing or diagnosing the ailments to which dogs are subject. Nostrums abound. They should be shunned. In bacterial, or microbic or contagious zymotic diseases, rare skill is necessary. If your child were ill, you would not hunt up a book on medicine. Even if you knew all that it contained, you might diagnose wrongly.

Nursing, as in the case of human beings, is "half the battle" in the majority of cases. In one of distemper, for instance, listen to no one if you can reach a veterinarian. You may be able to attend to a puppy's dentition or give your house pet a dose of castor oil, if it is dull, or functionally deranged, or dress a hurt,

58

but in serious cases depend on no one but an expert. There are some petty troubles that do not require expert treatment.

Parasites, such as fleas, may be got rid of in various ways. If they are found, determine if they exist elsewhere in the house. Grimalkin may have them, and if so, it, too, should have the same treatment. The pet's sleeping box and bedding must first be destroyed. Then it must have a bath, but, after it has been lathered with carbolic or tar soap, let the lather dry on and when it is nearly dry, be liberal with Persian Powder. When the coat is thoroughly dry, rinse it well and stow the dog away until dry again. A bi-chloride of mercury soap is as bad for fleas as for other vermin, only care should be taken not to let the animal lick the lather.

Worms and skin diseases, such as the mange, appear simple to deal with, but the reverse is the case. No medicine for these troubles should be given without the advice of an expert. The advice "do not trust to any one but an expert, and give no nostrums" is repeated. Where hydrophobia is suspected, sequester the dog and send for a veterinarian. In ninety-nine cases out of a hundred, the symptoms will be found to be due to epilepsy, worms or cerebral trouble. On no account kill a dog suspected of having rabies without consulting an expert. All sick dogs should be kept quiet until proper advice can be had. Under this head, advice may be given about the claws of your dog. In town they will grow long and sharp, and if neglected, hurt it. They should be snipped now and then with a wire cutter, but care should be taken not to cut off so much as to draw blood.

BREEDING AND CONSANGUINITY.

MINUTE directions in regard to breeding dogs have no place in this treatise. What has been said about purity of race and the folly of disregarding consanguinity is repeated. If, reader, you possess sire and dam, the responsibility for their progeny rests with you, in that you should be certain that each is blue blooded and not kin to the other; this is "out breeding." If to retrieve or perpetuate characteristics, you have to resort to remote consanguinity—"in breeding," —be prudent and take some advice from experts. Such "in breeding" may be necessary to secure coat, color, form and traits, but reckless "in breeding" is disastrous.

When the gyp is about to have her young, let her have some quiet place for her trouble and allow no person or animal to worry her. She will attend to her puppies in her own way. If there be trouble of any sort in delivery or in suckling, consult a veterinarian. Wean the puppies when they are six weeks old. You can readily learn how many whelps may be expected by naming your breed, and if more than four arrive, you should get rid of the surplus in some way.   Foster mothers are easily found and cats or mongrel dogs, deprived of their little ones, take kindly to puppies and make excellent wet nurses.

SOME OF OUR DOG BREEDERS.

IN England, dog breeders and owners are found in all classes—"from the Queen to the costermonger." The Prince of Wales and his mother are exhibitors at bench shows with their subjects, and Whitechapel snatches laurels from Belgravia and vice versa. Here we have the Belmonts, the Rutherfords, the Vanderbilts and others of the " Four Hundred " with Miss A. H. Whitney to judge their Pugs and their St. Bernards. An idea of the importance of dog raising and dealing may be had from the following partial list of what are known as kennels in this country and Canada and in which more than $1,500,000 are invested :

Associated Fanciers, Clementon, N. J.
Acme Kennels, 917 Chestnut St., Milwaukee, Wis.
Buckthorn Kennels, 100 Lexington Ave., New York City.
Brant Cocker Kennels, Brantford, Ontario, Canada.
Beaumont Kennels, 159 West 34th St., New York City.
Bleonton Kennels, Hempstead, L. I.
Caumsett Kennels, 9 West 35th St., New York City.
Chestnut Hills Kennels, Box 1630, Philadephia, Pa.
Cohannet Kennels, East Taunton, Mass.
Central Kennels, 340 Central Ave., Jersey City, N. J.

Chequasset Kennels, Lancaster, Mass.
Cook Kennels, Detroit, Mich.
Calumet Kennels, 2821 Emerald Ave., Chicago, Ill.
Contoocook Kennels, Peterborough, N. H.
Dunrobrin Kennels, Stanley, N. Y.
Erminie Kennels, Box 82, Mount Vernon, N. Y.
Elmwood Kennels, South Framingham, Mass.
Elm Kennels, Box 240, Westfield, N. J.
Far View Kennels, Dougan Hills, S. I.
Flour City Kennels, Rochester, N. Y.
Glendyne Kennels, Bristol, R. I.
Glenwood Kennels, Taunton, Mass.
Hornell-Harmony Kennels, Covert, N. Y.
Hempstead Farm Kennels, Hemsptead, L. I.
Halfpenny Brook Kennels, Glens Falls, N. Y.
Hospice Kennels, Arlington, N. Y.
Hudson River Kennels, Yonkers, N. Y.
Item Kennels, 1954 North 11th St., Philadelphia, Pa.
Killarney Kennels, 179 State St., Chicago, Ill.
Kilmarnock Collie Kennels, Box 1463, Boston, Mass.
Kildare Kennels, Box 1028, Pittsburgh, Pa.
Lake Shore Kennels, 418 Wabash Ave., Chicago, Ill.
Lothian Kennels, Stepney, Conn.
Mount Royal Kennels, Cote St., St. Antoine, Montreal, Canada.
Mohawk Indianola Kennels, Auburn Park, Ill.
McBeth Kennels, Massilon, Ohio.
Nahmke Kennels, East Patchouge, L. I.
North Fields Yorkshire Kennels, Salem, Mass.
Oriole Kennels, Youngstown, Ohio.
Park Kennels, 220 Canal St., Providence, R. I.
River View Kennels, 329 East 34th St., New York City.
Retnor Kennels, 173 Fifth Ave., New York City.
Rosecroft Kennels, 102 Chambers St., New York City.
Rochelle Kennels, Box 862, New Rochelle, N. Y.
Rockland Kennels, Nanuet, N. Y.

Regent Kennels, Cotonsville, Baltimore County, Md. •
Rockingham Kennels, 1263 Broadway, New York City.
Sunset Kennels, Bolingbroke, Ga.
Sea Moss Kennels, Glencoe, Ill.
Schoonhooven Kennels, Black Rock, Conn.
Somerset Kennels, Bernardsville, N. J.
Seminole Kennels, Chestnut Hill, Philadelphia, Pa.
St. Cloud Kennels, West Farm, N. Y.
Tunlaw Kennels, 2817 Q St., Washington, D. C.
Tiot Kennels, Norwood, Mass.
Wyoming Kennels, Melrose, Mass.
Wilton Kennels, 26 Chambers St., New York City.
Wentworth Kennels, 716 Genesee St., Utica, N. Y.
Woodhaven Kennels, 7 East 53d St., New York City.
Woodland Kennels, Woodstock, Ontario, Canada.
Woodbury Kennels, 135 South 8th St., Philadelphia, Pa.
Woodale Kennels, Woodside, Troy, N. Y.
Westminster Kennel Club, Babylno, L. I.

www.ingramcontent.com/pod-product-compliance
Lightning Source LLC
Chambersburg PA
CBHW022147090426
42742CB00010B/1419